D0930459

EXPECTATIONS
OF IMMORTALITY
IN LATE ANTIQUITY

The Aquinas Lecture, 1987

EXPECTATIONS OF IMMORTALITY IN LATE ANTIQUITY

Under the auspices of the
Wisconsin-Alpha Chapter of Phi Sigma Tau

by

A. HILARY ARMSTRONG

MARQUETTE UNIVERSITY PRESS
MILWAUKEE
1987

Library of Congress Catalogue Card Number: 87-60376

© Copyright 1987
Marquette University Press

ISBN 0-87462-154-2

For
MY WIFE DEBORAH

*who joined the company of the
blessed on December 10, 1986,
shortly after the completion
of this lecture.*

Prefatory

The Wisconsin-Alpha Chapter of Phi Sigma Tau, the National Honor Society for Philosophy at Marquette University, each year invites a scholar to deliver a lecture in honor of St. Thomas Aquinas.

The 1987 Aquinas Lecture, *Expectations of Immortality in Late Antiquity,* was delivered in the Todd Wehr Chemistry Building on Sunday, March 1, 1987, by A. Hilary Armstrong.

Professor Armstrong was born on August 13, 1909, in Sussex, England. He was educated at Lancing College, Sussex (1923-28), Jesus College, Cambridge (1928-32) and the University of Vienna (1932-33). He was Library Clerk in the Classical Faculty Library, Cambridge (1933-36) and Lecturer in Classics, University College, Swansea, S. Wales (1936-39). He was Professor of Latin and Greek at the University of Malta (1939-43); during the time of the great German bombardment and blockade of Malta the university continued to function. After the war he was Lecturer in Latin, University College, Cardiff (1946-50). He became Gladstone Professor of Greek in the University of Liverpool in 1950 where he remained until 1972 when he became Professor of Classics and Philosophy at Dalhousie University in Halifax, Nova Scotia where he remained until 1982. He has also been Visiting Professor at Manhattanville College

(1966) and at Villanova University (1979), where he also gave the Augustine Lecture in 1966.

Professor Armstrong was elected a Fellow of the British Academy in 1970 and received the Aquinas Medal from the American Catholic Philosophical Association in 1973. He has been a regular participant in the International Patristic Conference at Oxford, attended various international Neoplatonic conferences and, since 1984, the Eranos meetings at Ascona, Switzerland.

His publications include: *Architecture of the Intelligible Universe in the Philosophy of Plotinus* (1940), *Introduction to Ancient Philosophy* (1947), *Christian Faith and Greek Philosophy,* with R. A. Markus (1960), *Plotinus* (selections, 1953). He published a volume of collected papers, *Plotinian and Christian Studies,* in 1979 and is planning a second volume of papers for 1989. He has translated the *Enneads* of Plotinus for the Loeb Classical Library, *Plotinus* I-VII, the final two volumes of which are now in press. He was editor of and contributor to *Cambridge History of Later Greek and Early Medieval Philosophy* (1970) and also *Classical Mediterranean Spirituality* (Volume 15 of *World Spirituality,* 1986).

To Professor Armstrong's distinguished list of publications, Phi Sigma Tau is pleased to add: *Expectations of Immortality in Late Antiquity.*

EXPECTATIONS OF IMMORTALITY
The Late Antiquity

I

The subject I propose for this year's Aquinas Lecture is one suitable to my age and the studies in which I have spent my life. It would certainly have seemed worth considering to St. Thomas and other philosophers of our older tradition. But it is, from some strictly and narrowly philosophical points of view, a rather odd one, and neither it nor my treatment of it may seem appropriate for a philosophical lecture to some professional philosophers in the audience. If so, I apologize formally, but quite unrepentantly. I intend to consider a question which seems to me important, but to which, probably, no definite answer can ever be given of the sort which could be used as a basis for those large abstract generalizations which provide the materials for systematic overviews of human thought, religion and culture. The question is, to put it simply, "How much did expectations of an afterlife really matter to people in late antiquity, especially in the period from the second to the fourth centuries A.D. which I know best?" It is not "Did they in some sense believe in an after-life, and what was the discursively formulable content of their belief?" This might sometimes, though not always, be easier to answer. It is rather "How far was, not only what they believed, but what they felt and imagined about an after-life, strong enough to influence the way they behaved in this life and faced the always inescapable fact of bodily death?" In trying to answer this we are clearly moving into a very misty area, and any suppositions we may form about various answers must necessarily be very tentative. We shall be dealing with imponderables, feelings, imaginations and emphases. But if we do not attempt to do so we shall be very unlikely to make any real contact with the people of the age we are studying, even to the limited extent to which we can ever make contact with people of any past age, or to arrive at any sort of understanding of them which will help us to understand ourselves.

There is one great limitation on our study of expectations about the after-life in the ancient world which needs to be stated clearly at the beginning. It is generally recognized, at least in principle, by serious scholars who have worked in this field: though some, even eminent, scholars are sometimes rather inclined to forget it when they come to make generalizations about the period which they study. This is that nearly all the evidence which can be of any real help to us in giving even tentative answers to our question comes from a tiny minority of the population of the ancient Mediterranean world, the literate members of the upper classes. It is only from literature that we can get any ideas of the imponderables with which we are concerned, of the intimate interconnection of beliefs and imaginations, of vital differences of emphasis, of the feeling-tone of words and statements and images: and literature is only produced by the literate, and by a minority of the literate. Further, we only still have a small proportion of the writings which that minority of a minority produced: and if we are looking, as we should be, for the sort of deep reflection on life and death and what may come after death which may help us to understand, not only the ancients but ourselves and humanity in general, we shall only find it in a small minority of that minority of a minority, in the

philosophers and in those Jews and Christians
influenced by the Hellenic tradition of reflective piety. This is something which historians
of philosophy and religion should never forget. Our view of the past is so often distorted
by our own quite legitimate preoccupations.
As we study the few quite exceptional persons
who interest us we should always keep in
mind the vast assemblage of the inarticulate,
the predominantly peasant populations of the
old world from whom the minorities with
whom we are concerned emerged, by whom
they were continually surrounded, and from
whom they were not cut off in their ideas, still
less in their feelings and imaginations. We
need to remember this particularly carefully
when we are tempted to make those sorts of
large generalizations about regions and periods on which a good many philosophies of
history, or philosophies and theologies which
claim to understand history and to take it
seriously, are based. If we do, we shall be
disinclined to say things like "The Hellenistic
Age was sceptical and irreligious" or "Late
Antiquity was an extremely other-worldly
period."

The first was certainly a time when the articulate Hellenic minority, and, later, the edu-

cated upper-class Romans influenced by them wrote, and probably said, a great deal which is very sceptical and irreverent about gods and myths and cult, and, what particularly concerns us here, the after-life. But when we reflect, perhaps among the magnificent remains of the great oracular temple of Apollo at Didyma, on the many great temples built in that age and the splendid continuance of the traditional cults, of which we have ample evidence: or when we consider that the cult of Sarapis, probably put together by Ptolemy I from various Egyptian and Greek elements for political purposes, was a tremendous religious success throughout the Graeco-Roman world; the god aroused deep and passionate devotion down to the end of pagan cult in the fourth century A.D.: or when we observe, as historians of philosophy certainly should, that the most generally influential group of Hellenistic philosophers, the Stoics, are the most deeply pious of all Hellenic philosophical groups before the Neoplatonists: we shall begin to find the usual generalization rather silly and misleading.[1] As for the other-worldliness of late antiquity, as I have continued and tried to extend and deepen my study of the period during the last ten years

or so, I have more than once found occasion
to remind myself how misleading this generalization can be. A historian of religious thought
in this period is certainly concerned with
momentous changes of mentality and outlook
and with persons or groups who have made
a deep and lasting impression on very widespread later forms of piety and religious
reflection: and those persons and groups can
be described as in some sense "other-worldly":
though this term needs to be very carefully
applied, with many nuances and differentia-
tions which make it difficult to use as the foundation of any meaningful generalization. But
when one looks at these genuinely significant
people in the context of their own times one
soon discovers that their visibility is decidedly
low and their influences insignificant, and that
they cannot be regarded safely as at all representative. A great philosopher in late antiquity did not hold a chair in some imposing
institution of higher education like a medieval,
still less like a modern, university, for the
simple reason that there were no such institu-
tions. What we please to call "philosophical
schools" were small informal groups of a
master and a few disciples and friends with
no, or very little, institutional coherence or

continuity. This was certainly true of the "school" of Ammonius Saccas at Alexandria and the "school" of Plotinus at Rome. And as for the Gnostics, and in many parts of the Roman Empire before the fourth century A.D. more orthodox and mainstream Christians, they were insignificant sects which would be known and attractive to very few of the general population. If in the third century at Rome, in the time of Plotinus' residence in Rome when he was at the peak of his reputation, one had asked a personage of senatorial appearance in the Forum for directions to his lecture-room, the answer might well have been, "Plotinus? Never heard of him." And if one had asked someone of Oriental aspect, hung about with a few charms and amulets, in the Subura, the way to the nearest Gnostic chapel, he could easily have replied with something like, "What's Gnostics?" One would, indeed, have been very fortunate if one had casually encountered anyone in the street who could have directed one to the principal Christian church or the residence of the bishop of Rome. And one can arrive at the same sort of conclusion about the comparative insignificance in their own time of the people and movements whom we rightly consider significant if we look carefully at what survives of late antique art. Art is always one of the best guides we have to the mentality and sensibility of remote periods and peoples: and Peter Brown's observations that late antique and Byzantine art should properly be described as "inner-worldly" rather than "other-worldly" are most illuminating and fruitful to consider. But in commenting appreciatively on them I felt constrained to add, "of course we should not forget that a great deal of the surviving art of late antiquity, and even some survivng Byzantine art, is not "inner-worldly" or "other-worldly" but just worldly . . . And much late antique and medieval religion was of course equally worldly – the ordinary man in the Mediterranean area (and elsewhere), from peasant to emperor, has usually had a fairly down-to-earth and business-like attitude to the divinity coupled with a deep and genuine instinctive reverence for divine powers operative in his immediate environment."[2] As emperors are a reasonably visible group of generally intellectually and spiritually commonplace persons available to the student of late antiquity, it may be worth adding to this last remark that the general worldliness of

late antique religion can be well confirmed by
considering what we know of the religious
concerns of the general run of late antique
emperors, including Constantine I.

It may be objected at this point that on the
subject which concerns us here, that of expectations of immortality, we do after all have a
good deal of evidence about popular beliefs
and feelings from late antiquity. We know,
both from archeology and literature, a great
deal about burial customs, and we have a
great many epitaphs, though only a very small
proportion of those which must once have ex-
isted, and some monuments with elaborate
decoration the symbolism of which has been
extensively and liberally interpreted. I am not
altogether ignorant of this evidence and the
voluminous literature which it has generated.
But when one comes to consider how much
it can tell us about what the inarticulate mass
of the people of the ancient Mediterranean
not only thought but felt and imagined, hoped
and feared about life after death, considerable
doubts will soon arise, and these doubts are
shared by some of the greatest scholars who
have worked in this field. Cumont, whose
knowledge of the evidence was unrivalled,
expressed the difficulty of interpreting it

admirably in the introduction to his *Lux
Perpetua.*[3] The interpretation of burial customs is particularly difficult, especially when
one considers the elementary truth that in all
societies, but especially traditional ones like
that of the ancient Mediterranean world, the
main reason for following custom is simply
that it is customary to do so; one does things
with the dead because they have "always"
been done in one's family and its immediate
environment. Even when a change in custom
can be detected, its significance is not always
easy to see. Cumont, with others who have
followed him,[4] was inclined to make a great
deal of the change from cremation to inhuma-
tion in late antiquity. But another great
scholar, A. D. Nock, has given solid reasons
for not taking this too seriously as evidence
for any deep and general change in people's
expectations about the after-life in one of
his most impressive papers, "Cremation
and Burial in the Roman Empire."[5] And
when we turn from burial-customs to grave-
monuments, we certainly find that a limited
number of the more expensive of the scanty
and random selection of them which has survived display in their decoration a rich and
varied symbolism which, with the help of

literary sources, can be and has been interpreted as conveying a variety of often quite
positive beliefs about the after-life.[6] But when
we come to ask ourselves from the point of
view adopted in this lecture what this evidence can tell us about the general beliefs of
the mass of the peoples of the ancient Mediterranean world and how deeply felt these
beliefs were, how much their expectations of
immortality really meant to them, we shall
find that there are good reasons for extreme
caution and a considerable amount of agnosti-
cism: these reasons have been well stated in
another of Nock's great papers, "Sarcophagi
and Symbolism."[7] And even when we are considering the much greater and perhaps somewhat more representative collections of simple grave-inscriptions which we have, we shall
need to bear in mind continually the sensible
remarks of Martin P. Nilsson who, speaking
of the rather negative impression conveyed
by grave-inscriptions of the Hellenistic period,
says, "To demonstrate the unimportance of
belief in the underworld attention has been
drawn to the fact that it appears so little in
the grave-inscriptions: but one would be right
to remind oneself how little about Christian
beliefs in the resurrection, to say nothing of

the pains of hell, appears on the memorials of our churchyards," and reminds us a little later, "It was not for everyone to get a grave-inscription carved: one needed a bit of education and a certain amount of money."[8]

One can easily prove for oneself the truth of the first of Nilsson's remarks if one spends a certain amount of time in meditating among the tombs in the cathedrals or greater churches of Europe, as I have done while preparing this paper in the High Chancel and adjoining chapels of the great church of St. Laurence at Ludlow, where many of the nobility and gentry of the Welsh Marches are buried. Out of the forty epitaphs which I read in the course of my meditations, ranging in date from the sixteenth to the early twentieth century, only seven even mentioned a life beyond the grave. Judging from the epitaphs alone, one would have to assume that to those who composed them and saw to their erection, whether the deceased persons themselves or their friends, relations and spiritual and legal advisers, the landed properties, distinguished family connections and important positions held by the deceased meant considerably more than any hope of a blessed immortality or a joyful resurrection. Of course we are dealing here with an extremely well documented period, and plenty of information could be gathered from other sources which would enable us to form a better idea of these people's real hopes and fears about the afterlife. I do not think that any serious historian of English religious thought would rely very much on epitaphs, though we certainly have plenty of them, far fuller and more representative collections than we have for any place or period in late antiquity. But for late antiquity we have hardly any other documentation even for the hopes and fears of that small section of the inarticulate mass of the population who had enough money and minimal education to get themselves a monument. We should, therefore, beware of drawing any firm conclusions, negative or positive. In my meditations on the Ludlow tombs, just as I did not assume that because her epitaph says nothing about it, poor young Ambrosia Sidney did not die with a hope of immortality befitting her name, so I was not as sure that Dame Mary Eure died in a sure and certain hope of a joyful resurrection as the pious quotation from the Anglican funeral liturgy on her tomb would suggest.

The most, then, perhaps, that we can do

where the great majority of the Mediterranean peoples of late antiquity are concerned is to give some general ideas of the sort of vague expectations of immortality which were probably present in the thoughts and imaginations of many or most of them, arousing hopes and fears of varying intensity. Here we must remember that the old religion was not a credal or dogmatic religion and that there was no body of persons in the ancient religious establishment claiming to possess teaching authority. As long as one performed the sacred rites one could hold what beliefs one pleased and, unless one consorted with philosophers, an uncommon habit then as now, one would not be discouraged from quite happily holding several incompatible beliefs at once, and it seems likely that this is what many ordinary people did. There were, and probably always had been, people who had no expectations of immortality of any kind, for whom death was the end, though the number of people like this among the inarticulate masses was probably rather few. The old mythological Hades, the ghost-world under the earth, probably still survived with considerable vigour and the stories about it, kept alive by so much art and poetry, still had considerable power. This had been inconsistently combined from time immemorial with a different kind of belief about the dead in the earth, that they somehow lived on in their graves, under their native soil, present to their families and local communities to help or harm. This remained very powerful, and persisted long after the end of antiquity. If we search ourselves, we may still find traces of it in our own imaginations and deepest feelings. And then alongside all this, and probably strongly gaining ground in late antiquity, there was a quite different kind of belief about the dead, that they survived, not somewhere down in the earth, but up in the air, (this idea had been around since about the fifth century B.C.). This is the point where we have to be very careful about the evidence, and not to suppose that it indicates more than it does. There is not sufficient evidence to suppose that any large number of ordinary people shared the very precise ideas about different kinds of astral or celestial immortality which were held by various groups of the more reflective among the literate minority and can sometimes be detected in the symbolism of the grave-monuments. The most one can safely say is that there was a widespread belief that the dead were up in the sky somewhere, perhaps as some kind of star, perhaps enjoying themselves at an everlasting rather drunken party – this could also be located in the pleasanter regions of the old mythological Hades, which indeed could be transposed as a whole to the celestial regions, with its places of punshiment in the lower atmosphere.

II

Let us turn now to the articulate minority, and in particular to the minority of that minority who reflected deeply on death and the after-life. At least concentration on them will make the rest of this more like a normal philosophical lecture. The first group which I wish to consider is one which is very much still with us: the group of those whose beliefs about the divine, the world and human nature led them to regard death as the end, who had no hope or fear of a future life at all. This was by no means an entirely negative state of mind: the beliefs such people held were often very positive: few of them were atheists, and a good many, notably the Epicureans with their dogmatic rather fundamentalist religious faith, could not be described as agnostics. If we think for a little about their attitude to death, it will help us to understand something very important about ancient philosophy which separates it rather sharply from philosophy as it is generally understood in the contemporary, especially the English-speaking, academic world: and at least indirectly to appreciate the meaning of something which I hope we all know, that among our own contemporaries and friends many who are without any religious beliefs or expectations of immortality can manage the business of dying very well. As an introduction, I propose to consider three ancient uses of a pious commonplace which we have all probably at some time encountered in sermons or spiritual reading: that which says that we should take death seriously because we shall be dead so much longer than we shall be alive. My purpose in considering these very different uses of it is to show how detachable the serious consideration of death in a way which affects one's life can be from any particular belief or feeling about the after-life. My first example is from the *Antigone* of Sophocles. Antigone, giving her reasons why she should bury Polyneices in defiance of Creon's edict says:

It is good for me to die in doing this. I shall lie loved
with him who loves me when I have done my holy
crime. I have to please those below for longer than
those here. For there I shall lie for ever (72-76: my
own translation). [9]

One should not misunderstand this. It is a
grave mistake to read into Sophocles, or any
of the great fifth-century Attic tragedians,
any ideas, feelings or expectations about the
after-life other than those which belong to
that strange combination of acceptance of the
old stories about the sad Homeric ghost-world
and belief that the dead live on somehow in
their earth which I mentioned above. One
should not try to find anything else even in
the mysterious glory which pervades the last
scene of the *Oedipus at Colonus:* and the
feeling about death in the *Antigone* is darker.
None the less, even in the context of this dark
and depressing expectation of immortality,
Sophocles and his audience felt it appropriate
that the young princess of Thebes, setting out
to fulfill in love the law of duty to gods, family
and city which the king and head of her family
had violated, knowing what people would
think of her impertinence and that it would
lead to death, should put forward this commonplace in defence of her action.

The next example comes from a later poet with much more definite religious beliefs than Sophocles. It is taken from the great sermon on death in the third book of Lucretius *On The Nature Of Things,* of which the text is "Nil igitur mors est ad nos, nec pertinet hilum" "Death is nothing to us: it does not matter at all" (830). The Epicurean preacher says, as he draws to his close:

> In this way each man struggles to flee from himself: yet, despite his will, he clings to the self, which we may be sure, in fact, he cannot escape, and hates himself, because in his sickness he knows not the cause of his malady; but if he saw it clearly, every man would leave all else, and study first to learn the nature of things, since it is his state for all eternity, and not for a single hour, that is in question, the state in which mortals must expect all their being, that is to come after their death. (1068-1075: tr. Cyril Bailey). [10]

Here our commonplace is put forward as a reason for studying the nature of things, that scientific dogma may liberate us from the fear of death and what may come after it by assuring us that all those centuries after we are dead will mean no more to us than all those centuries before we were born. This takes us straight to the main theme of this part of the lecture, the philosophic preparation for death

which is independent of any particular belief
or disbelief about the after-life. But before
pursuing this further, we should note that our
flexible commonplace can be employed in less
serious contexts for considerably less elevated
purposes. At that appalling dinner-party in
the *Satyricon* of Petronius, when everyone
has reached a suitable degree of intoxication
for turning to lachrymose subjects, the host,
Trimalchio, after having his will read, pro-
ceeds to order his tomb, and justifies himself
for doing so by saying,

> It is quite wrong for a man to decorate his house
> while he is alive, and not to trouble about the house
> where he must make a longer stay (71: tr. Michael
> Heseltine.)[11]

Here the commonplace returns to the context
of the crudest, probably the most ancient, and
in an underground way most persistent belief
about life after death, that the dead live on
somehow in their graves and are very much
concerned about them. It is easy to observe
that this survived the official adoption of
Christianity. Trimalchio's successor in literature, Browning's Renaissance bishop ordering
his tomb in St. Praxed's church,[12] had plenty
of real-life predecessors, contemporaries and

successors, as a glance round any of the cathedrals and greater churches of Europe will
show.

The philosophic preparation for death,
which is for the ancients the most important
part of learning to live, needs to be considered
in the light of a wider understanding of the
nature of ancient philosophy. This understanding has always been available to (though
not always shared by) those who seriously
study the ancient sources; but it has been
given greater prominence and clarity recently
by the work of two fine scholars, Pierre and
Ilsetraut Hadot. It is the understanding that,
for most ancient philosophers, philosophy was
a comprehensive and extremely demanding
way of life, requiring, certainly, the intense
study of the whole of reality, but designed to
lead, not simply to what we should call an "intellectual" or "scientific" understanding of the
nature of things, but to the attainment of that
human goodness, including or consisting in
wisdom, but a transforming wisdom, which
alone can bring about human well-being. [13]
This understanding has inspired a great deal
of a recent volume which I have edited entitled *Classical Mediterranean Spirituality,* [14]
and is very well expressed by Ilsetraut Hadot

in one of the key articles in that volume.[15] She
says:

> It must be pointed out here that philosophy means
> something entirely different in Graeco-Roman anti-
> quity from what it does today. It is not in the first
> instance a systematic thought-structure *à la* Hegel
> intended to serve as the theoretical explanation of
> the world and the events of the world, but philo-
> sophy is above all an education towards a happy life,
> happy life here and not only in some hypothetical
> life after death, even if the latter was not always
> left entirely out of consideration . . . . Ancient
> philosophy is above all help with life's problems and
> spiritual guidance, and the ancient philosopher is
> above all a spiritual guide. Only secondarily, namely
> in so far as this is considered essential to spiritual
> guidance, is ancient philosophy a theoretical expla-
> nation of the world.[16]

These statements are of course intended to
correct an imbalance: and in view of the
amount which has been written, and conti-
nues to be written, which presents ancient
philosophy as an exclusively intellectual, theoretical, system-building or system-demolishing
activity, their emphasis is justified. But those
of us who share this understanding of the
ancients need to continue to remember that
they pursued their secondary activity of ex-
plaining the world with such intelligence,
vigour and enthusiasm, that they laid the

foundations of all later Western philosophy and science, and that indeed it sometimes became for them in practice primary, and led to a too theoretical, abstract and over-intellectualized view of the nature of things: though perhaps this is more true of lesser philosophers and of mediaeval and post-mediaeval derivatives from the ancient traditions. But it does amply justify the continuing study of the ancients from points of view very far from the moralistic, pious, and even "mystical" ones which those of us who have come to understand ancient philosophy as ancient spirituality are inclined to adopt.

On the subject of philosophic preparation for death with which we are concerned, Ilsetraut Hadot again puts the essentials very well. She says:

> The content to which the spiritual guidance of the Hellenistic schools of philosophy refers . . . can be characterized by two formulae – "learning to live" and "learning to die" where the latter formula can be regarded as the logical presupposition of the former . . . . Every philosophical tradition of antiquity wishes to teach its adherents how to die and how to overcome the fear of dying. [17]

She establishes and explains, with sufficient evidence from all periods of ancient philosophy, that the primary purpose of the intense

meditation on the last things practiced and
commended by the philosophers is not to pre-
pare us for any sort of life after death. It will
certainly ensure that we shall die well. But
what is important is that the detachment from
the pursuit of worldly goods, the liberation
from fears and passionate obsessive desires
produced by seeing their transitory objects
in the light of death, will enable us to live well
here and now. This is why "learning to die"
is important for all the philosophical traditions. It is, as we have seen, as important for
the Epicureans who dogmatically denied any
life after death as it is for the Platonists who
had strong expectations of immortality; and,
perhaps more significantly, it is equally important for the very large number of reflective
persons in between whose positions were a
good deal less definite. It is of central importance in the spiritual practice of the Stoics,
some of whom believed in some kind of limited
survival after death and others did not or
were agnostic; for most of them the matter
does not seem to have been of great importance. We can see very clearly here how the
ancient philosophers' experience of time and
history, and consequently their whole consideration of the purpose of human life, was

present-dominated, not future-dominated.[18]

This observation turns out still to have a good deal of relevance when we turn to examine more closely the attitudes to the after-life of those very other-worldly persons (as is generally supposed), in whom their whole school tradition generated a strong expectation of immortality, the Neoplatonists, Plotinus and his successors. If we concentrate in studying them on our main question, "How much did the expectation of immortality really matter to them? How far did their looking forward to an after-life really dominate or determine their whole way of living and thinking?" we shall find that the answer is not quite what conventional accounts of Neoplatonic otherworldliness might lead us to expect. This is particularly true of Plotinus, whose unique greatness and the distinctive quality of whose thought becomes clearer to me the more I study him in comparison with his successors, Hellenic and Christian. Plotinus is always in intention a very good Platonist, faithful, though freely and independent-mindedly, to the Platonic tradition, as he understood it through his reading and above all through the teaching of his master, Ammonius. He certainly believed in the after-life as firmly as

Plato could have wished. He devoted a treatise (IV 7 [2]) early in his writing period to the defense of the Platonic doctrine of the immortality of the soul against rival schools; he assumes it throughout the *Enneads,* and fully accepts the doctrines of rewards and punishments in the other world, and of reincarnation, including reincarnation in animal and plant forms (he speaks of people who lived so vegetable a life that "they took care to turn themselves into trees").[19] But when we come to look closely at what he has to say on the subject, and in particular when we look for evidence for a passionate interest in the subject, a dominating and consuming desire to be delivered from this life into a future life of perfect happiness in the spiritual world, we find, I think, something rather different. He does not seem to be primarily concerned to maintain that the next life is everything and this life is nothing in comparison, though he does repeatedly make proper Platonic, *Phaedo*-style, remarks of this sort, generally rather incidentally. His most powerful conviction, which he is intensely concerned to bring others to see, is the pre-eminent dignity of Soul. It is in this context that the question of immortality becomes important: this is as true of the closing section of his polemical treatise on immortality (IV 7) where he gives a positive exposition of his own version of the Platonic doctrine as it is elsewhere: it is impressively apparent in chapter 10, which ends with the astonishing image of the living gold hammering away its own dross. In the great protreptic exhortation to awake to our own true dignity in the treatise, *On The Three Primary Hypostases* (V 1 [10] 2), parts of which so deeply impressed St. Basil and St. Augustine, [20] what we are to awake to is that we are Soul, belonging to the third Divine hypostasis which is in continual present contact with the higher spiritual world of Intellect and that ultimate source and goal which we inadequately call the One and the Good. In the "ascents of the mind to God" of his great anti-Gnostic work, [21] and the treatise, *How the Multitude of Forms Came into Being and On the Good* (VI 7 [38]), what we are being called to is an experience immediately accessible in this life. The spiritual-intelligible for Plotinus is everywhere (V 8 [31] 7, V 9 [5] 13): the One is always immediately present (V 5 [32] 12). He certainly hopes after death for a vision and union which will be continuous and unimpeded as it cannot be in this life (VI 9 [9] 10).

But his emphasis is always on that difficult possibility of awakening and liberation into the divine which is human fulfilment here and now. And this is for him a possibility which is always realized, even though we are not conscious of it, at the highest or deepest level of ourselves. It is the constant conviction of Plotinus, expressed in his writings from the early treatise IV 8 [6] to the late I 4 [46] and I 1 [53] that "we do not altogether come down," that something in us always remains "above." He says in his account of the descent of human souls in the great work, *On Difficulties About the Soul:*

> But the souls of men see their images as if in the mirror of Dionysus and come to be on that level with a leap from above: but even these are not cut off from their own principle and from intellect. For they did not come down with Intellect, but went on ahead of it down to earth, but their heads are firmly set above in heaven. [22]

It is because of this conviction that in the treatise, *On Eternity and Time,* we can be invited to "go down from eternity to the enquiry into time, and to time, for there our way led us upwards, but now we must come down in our discourse, not altogether, but in the way in which time came down." [23] Plotinus sums up his assurance that what really matters for human well-being is the presence of eternity to us now and our presence in eternity now in the short treatise, *On Whether Well-Being Increases with Time* (I 5 [36]): his answer to the question in the title is, "No." This experience of presence seems to be dominant throughout the *Enneads* and is one of the characteristics of the philosophy of Plotinus (the other being his insistence, also based in his experience, that the Good, though most intimately present, is absolutely beyond all speech and thought) which gives it its peculiar strengthening and liberating power and capacity for fruitful development in more than one direction.

When we turn from Plotinus to his devoted friend and disciple, Porphyry, we are conscious of a very considerable difference of tone and emphasis as regards the expectation of immortality. The formal differences of doctrine between the two are perhaps not very great, and would certainly not have seemed so to either of them. Porphyry, it would appear, may have insisted more radically on the unity of Soul with the higher divine hypostases, Intellect and the One, and at the same time been rather more hesitant than his master

on the question of whether something of us
always remains above (the evidence here is
not easy to interpret). He certainly never lost
the strong sense of present eternity, though
his experience of it may have been less vivid
and compelling than that of Plotinus. This is
something which Neoplatonism has never lost,
and which has given it a great deal of its
abiding force and attractiveness. Iamblichus
and the Hellenic Neoplatonists who followed
him differed, as is well known, very sharply
from Plotinus and, as they generally consider,
Porphyry, on the question of the undescended
higher soul or self: for them human souls
altogether come down into this world. But
their wholly descended souls still had in them
and with them the whole hierarchy of benefi-
cent higher powers most intimately and immediately present, and with and in them the
immediate light and presence of the Good.
This is finely expressed by Proclus in the
passage of his *Commentary on the Timaeus*
where he adopts and develops the thought of
Iamblichus on prayer.[24] But even though
Porphyry retains the sense of divine presence
and so the possibility of human liberation into
the divine and human fulfilment here and
now, his expectation of immortality was much

stronger and more anxious than that of Plotinus. He seems to have been very seriously
concerned to escape from this world and the
body. Disembodiment was a matter of great
importance to him, and, alone among Neoplatonists, he believed in the possibility of permanent disembodiment, total escape from
body, for the spirit of the philosopher. Plotinus does not seem to have been very inter-
ested in the matter, and quite prepared to
envisage periodic returns of the soul to the
body.[25] The later Hellenic Neoplatonists defi-
nitely taught that all human souls must return
to the body at least once in every cosmic cycle,
and probably in the case of most of them a
good deal oftener.[26] And in considering
Neoplatonic attitudes to body and disembodiment we need to remember that for most of
the Neoplatonists escape from the earthly,
animal, body did not mean passage to a totally
bodiless condition: we may have also astral
or celestial bodies, which are no impediment
to the soul, and our embodiment in these may
be everlasting.[27] And perpetual embodiment
was for all of them, including Plotinus, the
lot of the divine World-Soul and the gods who
are the great parts of the material cosmos,
the heavenly bodies and the earth: and their

embodiment was a condition of the exercise of their proper divine powers and in no way a hindrance to their full enjoyment of divine life: though the gods of the purely spiritual or intelligible world rank higher, the state of the embodied gods is divinely satisfactory and shows that an ideal permanent relationship of soul and body exists in the material cosmos which is the best possible image of the intelligible. Augustine was well aware of this Platonic tradition, and uses it powerfully against Porphyry's extremism in the *City of God*. [28]

Andrew Smith in his excellent study of Porphyry[29] gives a very good account of the differences of tone and emphasis between him and Plotinus and offers some very probable reasons for them. He suggests that Porphyry's hesistant and melancholic temperament made it difficult for him to share completely his master's assurance of the possibility of attaining eternity here and now: and also that his greater concern for the religious life of ordinary men, the need to provide a way to God for those who were not philosophers, led him to place greater emphasis on the historical element and the importance of bodily death as an escape from the impediments which in ordinary earthly life obstruct the quest for enlightenment, liberation and salvation. The conclusion of the first part of Smith's book is worth quoting here, as it is highly relevant to our main subject. He says:

> For Porphyry, then, there is sufficient reason for desiring ultimate release even for the philosopher since the restrictions imposed by the body are considered by him to be a serious impediment, even at times an insurmountable obstacle, in attaining the goal. The doctrine of release reasserts once again the historic element as an important factor in the philosophic life and inevitably returns to natural death the importance it had lost in Plotinus. In so far as Porphyry tempers the extreme formulation of Plotinian spiritual transcendence we could claim that he shows a return to primitive Platonism. But perhaps it would be more correct to stress the uniqueness of Plotinus. I have hinted in these pages that personal and practical achievement played a great part in the formation of the philosophy of Plotinus and Porphyry. Personality seems to be one of the most important factors in the realm of contemplative metaphysics. Plotinus led Porphyry in philosophical thought. We also recall that he led him out of the trough of despair which almost brought him to suicide. [30]

In assessing Porphyry's other-worldliness and the importance of the expectation of disembodied immortality we should also take into account a tendency to extremist over-simplification which Heinrich Dörrie[31] detects in his doctrine of the soul. Everything is reduced to the schema *henosis-merismos:* movement towards unification is altogether good and movement towards division and multiplicity is altogether bad. It seems to me useful to bring this together with another interesting observation of Smith's when he is comparing Plotinus, Porphyry and Iamblichus at the end of his book "Is it not possible that, in the final experience of the divine, Iamblichus is as close to Plotinus, if not closer, than Porphyry? Iamblichus clearly distinguished human reasoning and transcendent *noesis* attained with the help of theurgy. Porphyry sometimes gives the impression that contemplation is a continuation at a higher level of abstract reasoning. Whatever Plotinian *noesis* is it is not simply abstract thought. It is an experience, and one feels that Iamblichus was familiar with it."[32] If we do this and take into account what has already been said, something seems to me to emerge about the distinctiveness of Porphyry which is not only relevant here, but may be of general interest to historians of philosophy: though I would not be too dogmatic about it, and do not suppose that it explains everything. In my reading about what is taken to be, and often strongly criticized and reacted against as being, "Platonism" in the West, I often find that it seems to be a rather different kind of philosophy and religion from that with which I am familiar in Plotinus and in the Hellenic Neoplatonists after Iamblichus, a philosophy and religion characterized by a sharp otherworldliness leading to a passionate aspiration to a totally disembodied immortality and a quite congruous sort of disembodied and abstract intellectualism. Now, in so far as we can reconstruct Porphyry's position as distinct and differing from that of other Neoplatonists, this seems to me to fit him rather well. And, in view of Porphyry's undoubted influence on earlier Western Platonism, I am inclined to wonder whether both Platonism and the understanding of what Platonism is in the West, from Augustine to our own times, have had a stronger and more distinctive Porphyrian colour than we have realized.

In general, it appears that the Neoplatonists were in accord with the whole ancient philosophical tradition of the practice of death in that their experience and their concerns and purposes were present- rather than future-dominated. What is primary for them is the sense of belonging to Soul, to which and in

which the higher divine realities are immediately present here and now in this life. To
become fully awake to this belonging and this
presence, and to help others to become so, is
the main task of the philosopher, and it is by
this awakening and awareness that it becomes possible to attain the fulness of human
well-being here and now in this world, to
reach the goal of *Eudaemonia*. They certainly
expected that after death their souls would
be less impeded in their vision of and union
with the divine realities. But they worshipped,
in their due order and degree, perennially embodied gods who, though embodied, enjoyed
the fulness of divine well-being; and most of
them expected to return periodically to life
in the body to carry on their vocation as souls
of communicating goodness to the material
world. Proclus, indeed, teaches in his commentary on the *Alcibiades*[33] that the best
souls may descend into bodies more often
than they need because of that generous
desire to communicate goodness which he
calls *erōs*. And how much the desire to escape
to a purely spiritual immortality mattered to
them seems to depend very much on the
strength of their experience of present eternity and of their feelings about the evils of

life in this world; and the strength of these may be due very often to quite unreligious and unphilosophical causes. Porphyry stands rather apart from other Neoplatonists in the intensity of his desire for disembodied immortality and his belief that permanent disembodiment is possible for a philosopher; in this he is closer to the more pessimistic Platonists and Pythagoreans of the preceding century, especially to the Platonizing Pythagorean or Pythagoreanizing Platonist, Numenius, whose influence was considerable. And in his case we must certainly take his temperament into consideration. Plotinus on a well-known occasion attributed his passion for death to too much black bile.[34] But even Porphyry never goes beyond the limits of Platonism by denying that this world is good and that souls have their work to do in it, and that divine souls work in it continually. And he too shared in the experience of present eternity, though with less intensity than Plotinus.

III

When we turn to the Christians of our period we shall naturally assume that the clarity and intensity of their expectations of immortality

will turn out to be much greater than that of
the non-Christian masses of the peoples of the
Empire or of the few among them who were
articulate and reflective. And to a considerable extent this assumption is justified. We
are dealing, to begin with, with much more
organized and compact groups of people, uni-
fied, in spite of all the deep divisions apparent
among them from the beginning, by belief in
a common doctrine; and the doctrine mattered
more to them than doctrine had ever done to
any groups of pious people in the ancient
world, and those who taught it had a much
greater authority in their communities than
any philosophers had ever been able to claim
or exercise. And the expectation of immortality was central to this teaching and to the
faith and hope which inspired it and which it
inspired because Resurrection was central to
it. St. Paul in his first letter to the Corinthians
set the tone, "If our hope in Christ has been
for this life only, we are the most unfortunate
of all people" (I Corinthians 15, 19: English
Jerusalem Bible translation). This intense
looking forward to the risen life after death
was strengthened and confirmed for Christians
by the fact that at least the devout among
them tended to see this earthly life in very

dark colours. It may indeed be that the strongly eschatological movement of Jewish faith within which Christianity originated developed in a context of deep disillusionment about the present state of God's people on earth and loss of hope about any triumphant future for them in this present world. Some most interesting observations on this have recently been published by Martha Himmelfarb.[35] But, whatever emphasis should be laid on this, it is certainly true that Christians of the early centuries of our present era shared the dislike of this present world and sense of discomfort in an earthly body which, though they should not be made the basis of too sweeping generalizations, were certainly widespread among articulate and reflective religious people. E.R. Dodds describes them well in the first chapter of his *Pagan and Christian in an Age of Anxiety*.[36] Mainstream Christians were certainly on the side of the Platonists against the pessimistic Gnostics in insisting that the material cosmos was good and made by the good God. But like both Platonists (in varying degrees) and Gnostics they felt themselves strangers and pilgrims in this world, whose true home, where they really belonged, was another and higher one. And the disjunction and contrast between the two worlds was made much sharper for the Christians because they so much projected their higher world into the future; it was for them the kingdom to come, the *New* Jerusalem. Here we encounter a future-dominated experience of time and history in contrast to the present-dominated experience of the Hellenic philosophers. This is one reason why for many Christians this world, so sharply separated from the next, seemed even darker and more horrible than it did to the more pessimistic Platonists and why their attitudes to worldly life and to the body and to sex were often rather difficult to distinguish in practice from those of the most alienated Gnostics. This kind of disjunction and its concomitant eager looking forward to the life after death brings Christians closer to Porphyry than to any other Neoplatonist: and at this point I find it interesting to reflect that a rather Porphyrian kind of sharply other-worldly Platonism slipped comparatively easily into the Christian tradition, not, perhaps, altogether to the advantage of either Platonism or Christianity: this of course in the West was mainly due to its qualified acceptance and severely critical but on the whole, for its time, remarkably fair and friendly assessment by Augustine. On the other hand, in the Greek-speaking Christian East the more world-affirming, strongly liturgical and sacramental, even, if one uses the word, as it often is used, in a loose, not theologically precise sense, incarnational Platonism of the great Hellenic Neoplatonists of Athens was, in spite of its, in the end not inconsiderable, influence on Christian thought, regarded by Christians with intense hatred, springing, I suspect, from a certain latent fear. This is all the more remarkable when one considers that here the anti-pagan hysteria of the solidly established Christendom of the Empire was focussed on a very small group of mostly interrelated devout and scholarly gentlemen and ladies living inconspicuously in a venerable university town of no great contemporary importance. There is much more to be said about this from various historical, philosophical and theological points of view, but the contrast does seem to me to be worth considering.

How far this future-directed experience and attitude, this passionate expectation of the world to come, persisted among Christians in later centuries and still has any real strength

today, is an interesting and complex question,
which would lead us far beyond any reason-
able limits of this lecture if I even attempted
a preliminary sketch of the variety of answers
which would have to be given to it according
to the differences of the periods, places and
social groups concerned. It does seem to me,
however, in my present religious environment,
that it has very little strength among English,
and perhaps generally among European, Christians today: though some theologians and
preachers do their best to work it up, more
often in some more or less secularized than
in its original and authentic eschatological form. In an ordinary Eastertide sermon
preached before an ordinary congregation
which I heard not long ago in St. Laurence,
Ludlow, the young preacher said, rather
quaintly but forcibly, "The Future has no
teeth for most of us"; and most of his congregation, and most other congregations, would
simply accept that as true. This has led me
to consider that what I have just said about
the Christians of the first centuries, basing
my account on an authoritative text from St.
Paul, requires a good deal of qualification. Did
St. Paul really do himself and his converts
justice in that fine rhetorical flourish quoted

above? Was Christian life in this world so mis-
erable for them that they had to look forward
so intensely to the resurrection? There is
surely a great deal of evidence in the Pauline
Epistles and elsewhere that it was not so.
Christians from the beginning were sustain-
ed as much as the great philosophers by the
sense of the divine presence here and now in
this world, by the awareness of the living
Christ with and in them in this present life
and bringing by his presence an intense joy
and confidence which did not depend on expectations of a future life; and it was precisely
because of this sense of presence that they
looked forward eagerly to the resurrection.
And this, surely, was more and more true of
later Christian generations as the original
authentic eschatological experience faded and
the expectation of the Parousia receded.

At this point it will be interesting to consider what we can discern of the part played
by expectations of a future life in stimulating
and sustaining the courage of the martyrs,
who of all people would seem to show most
clearly by their attitude to death that these
expectations really mattered to them. There
are certainly some of whom this is true. Ignatius of Antioch expresses it most powerfully

of all in his letter to the Romans. It seems
particularly clear in those who deliberately
offered themselves for martyrdom, like that
crowd of Christians in Asia of whom Tertullian speaks in the *Ad Scapulam* (5) whom the
magistrate regarded as suicidal. And the
stories told by Eusebius about the young Origen's behaviour in the persecutions (*Historia
Ecclesiastica* VI, 2, 3-6: 3, 3-5) show very well
how for many Christians this passionate pursuit of martyrdom was appropriate conduct
for a holy man. There is one very distinctive
group of these seekers after martyrdom who
merit rather more attention than they have
generally received. These are the Christians
who ensured their passage through death to
life eternal by violent attacks on pagan shrines
and religious celebrations. Henry Chadwick
has recently sketched the history of the best
documented of these, in North Africa. He
shows that the groups later called Circum-
cellions, who called themselves Agonistici,
predate the Donatist schism and represent,
not anything distinctively schismatic, but the
ferociously uncompromising spirit of the ancient Church of North Africa. He gives a vivid
account of their proceedings, based on evidence from St. Augustine.

In more than one passage Augustine specifies that
the Agonistici specialized in causing the maximum
disruption at pagan festivals, where they used to
mount an unstoppable charge upon the band of musi-
cians, the *symphoniaci,* who were a normal feature
of pagan religious occasions. The Agonistici made
a concerted rush, and smashed the instruments of
the orchestra. They would also assault *iuvenes,* the
collegium of young men who used to parade in full
armour at religious festivals. The young pagans
made use of their swords, and despatched their
assailants . . . . The militants greatly prized their
martyrs and built shrines to their memory – cellae –
to which on the anniversary they would return . . .
to sing hymns in honour of their heroes and cele-
brate, *more africano,* in plentiful potations of wine.
Since the time and the place presumably coincided
with the pagan festivals at which the marytydoms
first occurred, the confrontations must have tended
to be annual and so a recurrent cycle. Hence their
cry "Deo Laudes". They were echoing the dying
words of Christian martyrs like Cyprian.[37]

This sort of behaviour, however, was not
generally approved by the Church.[38] It was
not till the Christians had the big battalions
on their side, after the conversion of the
Emperors, that bishops led mobs to destroy
pagan shrines. And in many of the authentic
acts of the martyrs the tone is much soberer
than in St. Ignatius, and other reasons for
courage and endurance, loyalty to Christ and
the sense of his presence with the martyrs

here and now, seem as important as the expectation of heaven. And in any attempt at general assessment of the attitudes of Christians we should not forget the very large numbers who illustrated the point that the religion of the great majority of people in this supposedly "other-worldly" period was decidedly mundane, and of moderate importance to them, by apostasy, or by making convenient arrangements with the authorities to avoid death for the faith without formal apostasy. We need to set against Tertullian's crowd clamouring for martyrdom in the *Ad Scapulam* Cyprian's crowd of eager apostates in the *De Lapsis* (8, 9).

How much difference did their distinctive belief in the resurrection of the body, or the flesh, make to the intensity and fervour of the hopes and fears of Christians about the future life? How much did it really make it matter more to them? I am inclined to think, tentatively, that it made less difference than the continual passionate insistence on the doctrine by apologists, preachers and theologians might lead us to believe. There is of course no possibility of doubt about the vigour with which the doctrine was preached or the sincerity with which it was believed by most

Christians: but the question of how much it mattered, how deeply they felt about it, is a rather different one. There was, no doubt, a great deal of rather naive and childlike looking forward to the risen life in the body: one of the most attractive expressions of this, obviously written with enjoyment and loving expectation of the prospect, is to be found in the last book of St. Irenaeus *Adversus Haereses,* especially in those chapters where he depends upon the teaching of the Elders and Papias, who had seen John the Lord's disciple (*Adversus Haereses* V, 33-35). Of course, his description refers to the Millenium, a future age which though long and glorious will in its time pass away: when he comes to the final and everlasting state of the blessed, Irenaeus wisely says very little, and bodily delights and beauties recede rather into the background. But when one considers, as one must, what the reflective and articulate minority of Christians have to say about the risen life, one becomes aware that they find it rather difficult to fill the hope of bodily resurrection with much solid content, to present much that could arouse joyful expectation. When I attempted some years ago to consider the part allotted by the Fathers to the risen body in

the Beatific Vision which is to constitute our
final blessedness, I found that, when anything
was said about it at all, this part was a decidedly modest one.[39] I felt sometimes that
these good Christian writers were rather in
the position of people who have, for excellent
reasons, invited a dearly loved relative to
come and live with them, and are rather des-
perately trying to find some satisfying occu-
pation for her about the house. The solution
preferred in the East, that either a most important part or the whole of the Vision of God
consists of the contemplation of the glorified
body of Christ with the eyes of the risen body,
if it is rightly understood as by no means
excluding, but involving and containing, the
vision of the incorporeal Trinity, is indeed a
very Christian solution. But it may seem
somewhat superfluous to bring in the body in
this sort of way to a Platonist who has learnt
from Plotinus, and from William Blake, that
all in the corporeal world, the world perceived
by the senses, exists more authentically, and
in the eternal glory of which our corporeal
arts sometimes manage to convey a gleam,
in the inner world of spirit and imagination.
Waking to glory, for a Platonist of this tradition, would be waking up in this inner world

so understood. And if the resurrection of the body could be understood in terms of this sort of awakening to discover all the goodness and beauty we have loved in bodies and bodily experience in their glorious eternal archetypes (including archetypes of individuals where these are necessary for the perfection of the glory), and emphasis on it could be taken as necessary to counteract more disembodied and over-intellectualized accounts of the spiritual world and the future life and the vision of God; then the doctrine might come to seem more attractive and acceptable to at least a few more people than it generally does nowadays. But little foundation, I think, could be found for this in the teachings of the Fathers and the early church. Those Christian thinkers influenced by Platonism, from Origen to Augustine, envisaged heaven and the vision of God in a more unbodily and intellectual way than sometimes emerges in the visions of Plotinus: and, when they came to preach the doctrine of the resurrection of the body, generally, with the exception of Origen, whose views were not approved, did so in terms of some sort of corporeal resuscitation. I am left with the feeling that, whether it is applied to this period or his own or later periods, there is an uncomfortable grain of truth in Avicenna's vigorous assertion that the Muslims do this sort of thing much better than the Christians: that the account of heavenly bliss in corporeal terms given in *Sura* 55 of the Koran is much more attractive to ordinary people than anything the Christians can come up with; both, of course, in his view, are incredible to the philosopher. [40]

We should not, of course, forget, when considering the part played by the hope of resurrection in Christian expectations of immortality, that the form of the belief most generally found in the Fathers, in which an immortal soul, already in some sense with God and enjoying at least a measure of beatitude, is rejoined at the General Resurrection by its risen body, was not, probably, the oldest form in which the doctrine was preached and believed and was not universally held in the period which we are considering. The very clear-cut view of the Arab Christians refuted by Origen (Eusebius, *Hist. Eccl.* VI 37), that the soul dies and is dissolved with the body and comes alive again along with it at the resurrection, which had Jewish antecedents, seems to have been traditional and persistent among Christians of the Semitic-speaking

East, and so has a good chance of being near to the original preaching of resurrection. And even when things were not so definite, and some survival of souls in an intermediate state, stored away somewhere to await the general resurrection, was believed in (and this was very widespread) the view of the state of these souls could vary considerably, from something which could be spoken of as Paradise to a long sleep or unconsciousness; this last view – so natural, and often so welcome, an understanding of death – certainly affected the language of many Christian epitaphs and even of the Latin Liturgy. [41] This kind of belief in resurrection has shown some tendency to persist among Christians in later centuries, and has revived vigorously recently. The Semitic doctrine alluded to above is of course quite fashionable among modern theologians. [42] And belief in the condition of souls in the "intermediate state" as a sleep is to be found sometimes among the learned Tractarian divines of 19th century England, who based their teaching solidly on the early Church of the Fathers. Since they and their followers are more accessible to us, in the sense that we have much more evidence about their feelings and expectations than we have for ordi-

nary Christians of the early centuries, they
may help us to understand a certain oscilla-
tion in hope and desire which is likely to occur
where the faith held is that in a sleep of death
followed by a waking in the body to everlasting life. The emphasis will sometimes be
on the sleep, the rest, the peace, and sometimes on the glorious awakening. This kind
of variation in feeling is best expressed by the
poets, and this group of austere, devout and
rigidly orthodox Christians, so consciously
close in their faith and devotion to the
Fathers, contained one very good poet, Christina Rossetti, who wrote several times on
this theme. In one of her best and best known
poems, *Rest,* both the sleep and the waking
are there, and one can feel where the emphasis lies:

> O Earth, lie heavily upon her eyes;
> Seal her sweet eyes weary of watching, Earth;
> Lie close around her; leave no room for mirth
> With its harsh laughter, nor for sound of sighs,
> She hath no questions, she hath no replies,
> Hushed in and curtained with a blessed dearth
> Of all that irked her from the hour of birth;
> With stillness that is almost Paradise.
> Darkness more clear than noonday holdeth her,
> Silence more musical than any song;
> Even her very heart has ceased to stir;
> Until the morning of Eternity

> Her rest shall not begin nor end, but be;
> And when she wakes she will not think it long.[43]

I do not think it anachronistic or unreasonable to suppose that this superb sonnet may convey something of the deepest feelings of those early Christians who understood death and resurrection in terms of sleep and waking, whether they thought of the sleeping soul, in some dim, confused and very ancient way, as sharing the rest of the body in the grave, as the poet's imagination does here, or as reposing in some mysterious "receptacle": and I think it possible that the emphasis of feeling among those who believed like this may have quite often been where it is in the poem, on the peace of sleep rather than on the glorious awakening (in which I am sure they believed, as Christina Rossetti did). *In Pace* on the gravestones meant, I think, just what it said.

At the beginning of this lecture I said that I had chosen this subject because I considered it appropriate to my age. For the same reason, it seems suitable to conclude with some account of such tentative expectations of immortality as a lifetime of studies of the philosophy and religion of late antiquity have left me with. This will also serve the properly philosophical purpose of disclosing something, at least, of my personal bias and limitations, in a more positive and courteous way than a more abstract and polemical statement of them might do. The disclosure of bias and limitations is something which anyone who speaks or writes on philosophical or theological subjects should attempt, especially, though not only, those who follow, as I do, the tradition of the *non uno itinere,* that there are many paths, not one only, to the great mystery. On the Hellenic side, I find that I tend to go back to the archetypal figure of Hellenic philosophy, the Platonic Socrates, but the Socrates of the *Apology* rather than of the *Phaedo.* His speech after sentence is the most powerful, invigorating and helpful of all the ancient philosophical meditations on death. In its last part, addressed to those who had voted for his acquittal (39E-42A) he sets out the alternatives, and shows first, with unsurpassed power because so tersely and quietly, that if death is unconsciousness, a deep and dreamless sleep, then it is a great good. Then he passes to what may well have been his own faith, in some kind of personal conscious survival: and here he is convincing and helpful because his touch is so light; he clearly does not expect his hearers to take what he tells them about the next life too literally, but tells a story and makes a joke. All that is serious, and it is enough for him, is that we shall be with the great company of the departed and in the care of the gods. And his last words, which no-one who has read the *Apology* ever forgets, leave all questions open. They give room for doubt, and can therefore stimulate most strongly to hope.

On the Christian side my tentative expectations of immortality are more and more linked with the other icon which in Byzantine usage can bear the title *Anastasis,* "resurrection," which represents what we call the Harrowing of Hell, [44] and with the letters of a friend, the late Mother Maria Gysi, one of whose favorite icons it was. [45] The icon has the great advantage, from the point of view of a critical historian, that one does not have to worry too much about the history. Most, even conservative, theologians would not be greatly upset if one said that it was a symbolic picture rather than the representation of a historical event. It also has for me a distinct aura of universalism about it, which is satisfying to a deeply committed Origenist. I am not of course suggesting that this was in any way

the conscious intention of the iconographers,
liturgists or theologians at any time concerned with this great Christian symbol
(though one never quite knows. I once, in con-
versation with a Catholic bishop of unim-
peachable orthodoxy and distinctly conservative views on many subjects discovered that
he was privately convinced that Hell was
empty.). But it does convey a distinct impression that He gets them all out. Perhaps my
friend felt this too: there are several places
in her writings which suggest that she might
have done, above all three tremendous sen-
tences written in Holy Week 1953, when, as
an Orthodox nun, she would have been thinking about not only the icon but the Good Fri-
day evening office, the *Epitaphios Thrēnos,*
the *Dirge at the Tomb,* much of which is a
song of triumph at the *Anastasis.*

> Infinite hope for hell in that stillness of death. There
> are no enemies. He said it himself. [46]

In her last years, when she was engaged in
the work of dying slowly and painfully, she
wrote many letters to her friends about death
and the life to come, in which they find continual support and encouragement to hope.
The letters do not go into details about that

other world which she saw then so clearly, but show it to us as a place of unbounded liberation and all-welcoming love. I will end with a quotation from one of them, written to me:

> I am trotting along very quietly and peacefully on my way to the "heavenly Jerusalem" which for me, as for Plotinus, is very much the joy of total transparence to each other, and never again hedges and frontiers and unsurpassable barriers and infinite spaces to divide and uphold tidy divisions; and various sheepfolds. To break through all that with no longer arousing suspicion! . . . . the weariness of body is very hard to bear, and I must keep my heart vigorously still, and am usually just taking my thoughts off, and diving into what I call my "death-country" – which is the wide open land within, of love with no limits. [47]

Notes

1. I have recently begun to put together a little collection of prayers and spiritual readings from the ancient world as a contribution to a book to be issued in connection with *World Spirituality* (see n. 14). And in spite of my Platonic predispostions and increasing affection and respect for classical Greek religion, it is clear to me that a great deal of what must be considered for inclusion in a book of this kind will have to come from the Stoics.

2. Peter Brown, *The World of Late Antiquity* (London: Thames and Hudson, 1972) pp. 74 and 78. A. H. Armstrong, "Gnosis and Greek Philosophy" in *Gnosis,* ed. Barbara Aland et al. (Gottingen: Vandenhoek and Rupprecht, 1978) = A. H. Armstrong, *Plotinian and Christian Studies* (London: Variorum, 1979) XXI, p. 114, n. 60.

3. F. Cumont, *Lux Perpetua* (Paris: Geuthner, 1949) p. 2.

4. E.g., J. M. C. Toynbee, *Death and Burial in the Roman World* (London: Thames and Hudson, 1971) Ch. II.

5. A. D. Nock, "Cremation and Burial in the Roman Empire," *Harvard Theological Review* 25, (1932), 321-59 = A. D. Nock, *Essays on Religion and the Ancient World,* ed. Zeph Stewart (Oxford: Clarendon Press, 1972) I, 14 pp. 277-307.

6. F. Cumont, *Recherches sur le symbolisme funeraire des Romains* (1942); *Lux Perpetua* (1949) (see n. 3). J. M. C. Toynbee, *Death and Burial in the Roman World* (see n. 4).

7. A. D. Nock, "Sarcophagi and Symbolism," *American Journal of Archeology* 50 (1946) 140-170 = *Essays on Religion and the Ancient World* (see n. 5) II, 606-641.

8. Martin P. Nilsson, *Geschichte der Griechischen Religion* II (Munich: Beck, 1950) 220-21: my own translation from the German.

9. καλόν μοι τοῦτο ποιούσῃ θανεῖν. φίλη μετ' αὐτοῦ κείσομαι, φίλου μέτα, ὅσια πανουργήσασ'· ἐπεὶ πλείων χρόνος ὃν δεῖ μ' ἀρέσκειν τοῖς κάτω τῶν ἐνθάδε. ἐκεῖ γὰρ αἰεὶ κείσομαι·

10. quam bene si videat, iam rebus quisque relictis naturam primum studeat cognoscere rerum temporis aeterni quoniam, non unius horae, ambigitur status, in quo sit mortalibus omnis aetas, post mortem quae restat cumque, manenda (Lucretius, *De Rerum Natura* III 1071-5).

11. valde enim falsum est vivo quidem domos cultas esse, non curari eas, ubi diutius habitandum est.
(Petronius, *Satyricon* 71).

12. "The Bishop Orders his Tomb at St. Praxed's Church [Rome 15-]" in *The Poems of Robert Browning* (Oxford: University Press, 1928) pp. 134-6.

13. See P. Hadot, *Exercices Spirituels et Philosophie Antique* (Paris: Études Augustiniennes, 1981): but this understanding of ancient philosophy is now becoming quite widespread, though those scholars whose interests lie elsewhere, e.g., in logic or natural science, or who dislike, as many classical scholars do, anything with a religious flavour, quite properly do not always advert to it. A good example of modern philosophy in the ancient manner, firmly grounded in Platonism but thoroughly contemporary in its concerns, is Stephen R. L. Clark's *From Athens to Jerusalem: The Love of Wisdom and the Love of God* (Oxford: Clarendon Press, 1984; based on his 1982 Gifford Lectures).

14. New York: Crossroad, 1986: Volume 15 of *World Spirituality: An Encyclopaedic History of the Religious Quest.*

15. "The Spiritual Guide," op. cit. (n. 14) pp. 436-59, tr. Margaret Kirby.

16. Art. cit. (n. 15) p. 444.

17. Art. cit. p. 450.

18. For this distinction see Peter Manchester, "The Religious Experience of Time and Eternity," in *Classical Mediterranean Spirituality* (see n. 14) pp. 384-407: and for further reflections A. H. Armstrong, "The Hidden and Open in Hellenic Thought," in *Eranos* 54 (1985) (Frankfurt: Insel, 1987) pp. 114-125.

19. I 1 [53] 12; III 2 [47] 13; III 3 [48] 4; III 4 [15] 2 (καὶ ἦν αὐτοῖς μελέτη δενδρωθῆναι 23-24); IV 3 [27] 24.

20. See my note ad loc. in *Plotinus* V (Cambridge, MA. and London: Loeb Classical Library, 1984) pp. 14-15.

21. The work dismembered by Porphyry into the four treatises: III 8 [30]; V 8 [31]; V 5 [32]; II 9 [33], referred to by the Germans as the *Grossschrift* and entitled by V. Cilento in his edition (Florence: Le Monnier, 1971) *Paideia Antignostica*.

22. Ἀνθρώπων δὲ ψυχαὶ εἴδωλα αὐτῶν ἰδοῦσαι οἷον Διονύσου ἐν κατόπτρῳ ἐκεῖ ἐγένοντο ἄνωθεν ὁρμηθεῖσαι, οὐκ ἀποτμηθεῖσαι οὐδ' αὗται τῆς ἑαυτῶν ἀρχῆς τε καὶ νοῦ. Οὐ γὰρ μετὰ τοῦ νοῦ ἦλθον, ἀλλ' ἔφθασαν μὲν μέχρι γῆς, κάρα δὲ αὐταῖς ἐστήρικται ὑπεράνω τοῦ οὐρανοῦ. (IV 3 [27] 12, 1-5, tr. A. H. A.)

23. Καὶ τοίνυν καταβατέον ἡμῖν ἐξ αἰῶνος ἐπὶ τὴν ζήτησιν τοῦ χρόνου καὶ τὸν χρόνον· ἐκεῖ μὲν γὰρ ἦν ἡ πορεία πρὸς τὸ ἄνω, νῦν δὲ λέγωμεν ἤδη οὐ πάντη καταβάντες, ἀλλ' οὕτως, ὥσπερ κατέβη χρόνος. (III 7 [45] 7, 7-10, tr. A. H. A.). For the full significance of this see

Peter Manchester, "Time and the Soul in Plotinus," in *Dionysius* II (December 1978) 101-136, especially 134.

24. Proclus, *In Timaeum* II, 209-210 Diehl.

25. IV 4 [28] 3-5; V 7 [18] 1.

26. Proclus, *Elements of Theology,* props. 198-200; *In Timaeum* III, 275-279 Diehl; *In Alcibiadem* 32, p. 14 Westerink.

27. See E. R. Dodds, "The Astral Body in Neoplatonism," Appendix II of *Proclus: The Elements of Theology* (Oxford: Clarendon Press, 1963) pp. 313-321 for the complexities and variations of this doctrine.

28. Augustine, *City of God* XXII, 27-28.

29. Andrew Smith, *Porphyry's Place in the Neoplatonic Tradition* (The Hague: Nijhoff, 1974).

30. Op. cit., p. 80. The reference in the last sentence is to the episode which Porphyry describes in ch. 11 of his *Life of Plotinus.* He says "He came to me unexpectedly while I was staying indoors in my house and told me that this eagerness for death did not come from a settled rational decision but from a bilious indisposition (ἐκ μελαγχολικῆς τινος νόσου), and urged me to go away for a holiday" (tr. A. H. A.).

31. Heinrich Dörrie, "Die Lehre von der Seele," in *Porphyre* (Vandoeuvres-Geneve: Foundation Hardt, 1965) pp. 167-191.

32. Smith, op. cit. (n. 29), pp. 149-150.

33. See n. 26.

34. See n. 30.

35. Martha Himmelfarb, "From Prophecy to Apoca-
    lypse," in *Jewish Spirituality from the Bible Through
    the Middle Ages* (Vol. 13 [1986] of *World Spirituality*
    [see n. 14] ed. Arthur Green) pp. 145-165.

36. Cambridge: University Press, 1965.

37. Henry Chadwick, "Augustine on Pagans and Chris-
    tians," in *History, Society and the Churches, Essays
    in Honour of Owen Chadwick,* ed. D. Beales and G.
    Best (Cambridge: University Press, 1986) p. 15.

38. T. C. G. Thornton, "The Destruction of Idols – Sinful
    or Meritorious?" *Journal of Theological Studies* N. S.
    37, 1 (April 1986) pp. 121-129: Chadwick, art. cit. (n.
    37) p. 16.

39. A. H. Armstrong, "Gottesschau," in *Reallexikon für
    Antike u. Christentum* XII (Stuttgart: Hiersemann,
    1981) B. II, c. 2 coll. 15-18.

40. A. J. Arberry, *Revelation and Reason in Islam*
    (London: Allen and Unwin, 1957) p. 53.

41. The evidence on this is well collected in *Note
    Complémentaire* 35 (by Louis Canet) of Franz Cu-
    mont, *Lux Perpetua* (see n. 3) pp. 445-461 (cp. also
    N. C. 31, 436-443).

42. Cp. Maurice Wiles, *The Remaking of Christian Doc-
    trine* (London: SCM Press, 1974) *Appendix,* "The
    Resurrection of the Body," pp. 125-146: Stephen R.
    L. Clark, *The Mysteries of Religion* (Oxford: Basil
    Blackwell, 1986) Ch. 11. "Death and Immortality,"
    pp. 204-207: the whole chapter is an excellent discus-
    sion of contemporary views by a Christian Platonist
    philosopher.

43. The poem is to be found in most anthologies which contain 19th-century English verse: e.g. *Oxford Book of English Verse* ed. A. Quiller-Couch, No. 789: *New Oxford Book of English Verse* ed. Helen Gairdner, No. 675. On the religion of Christina Rossetti, see Georgina Battiscombe *Christina Rossetti* (London: Constable, 1981).

44. The supreme surviving representation of this in Byzantine art is the fresco in the apse of the *parecclesion* of the Church of the Chora (the *Kariye Djami*) in Constantinople, in which the redemption of Eve is, unusually, given equal emphasis with that of Adam. It is well reproduced on pp. 340-359 of Paul A. Underwood, *The Kariye Djami* III (Bollingen Series LXX [New York, Bollingen Foundation/ Pantheon Books, 1966]. There is a fine representation in the usual form in the recently restored mosaics of the west wall of the Basilica of Torcello in the Venetian Lagoon. Icons, both Greek and Russian, are very numerous.

45. Sister Thekla (ed.) *Mother Maria. Her Life in Letters* (London: Darton Longman and Todd, 1979), from which the following quotations are taken.

46. P. 118.

47. Pp. 114-115. For an application of this vision to Christian life and thought here and now see another letter written in the same year (1975): "Oh – let us at last have the faith released into freedom of movement of thought, and of love, unafraid and without defenses – how it then could blossom!" (p. 93).

Published by the Marquette University Press
Milwaukee, Wisconsin 53233
United States of America

#1 St. Thomas and the Life of Learning (1937)
    by John F. McCormick, S.J. (1874-1943)
    professor of philosophy, Loyola University.
    ISBN 0-87462-101-1

#2 St. Thomas and the Gentiles (1938) by Morti-
    mer J. Adler, Ph.D., Director of the Insti-
    tute of Philosophical Research, San Francisco,
    Calif.   ISBN 0-87462-102-X

#3 St. Thomas and the Greeks (1939) by Anton
    C. Pegis, Ph.D., professor of philosophy,
    Pontifical Institute of Mediaeval Studies,
    Toronto.   ISBN 0-87462-103-8

#4 The Nature and Functions of Authority (1940)
    by Yves Simon, Ph.D., (1903-1961) profes-
    sor of philosophy of social thought, Univer-
    sity of Chicago.   ISBN 0-87462-104-6

#5 St. Thomas and Analogy (1941) by Gerald B.
    Phelan, Ph.D., (1892-1965) professor of phi-
    losophy, St. Michael's College, Toronto.
    ISBN 0-87462-105-4

#6 St. Thomas and the Problem of Evil (1942) by
    Jacques Maritain, Ph.D., professor *emeritus*
    of philosophy, Princeton University.
    ISBN 0-87462-106-2

#7 Humanism and Theology (1943) by Werner
    Jaeger, Ph.D., Litt.D., (1888-1961) Univer-
    sity professor, Harvard University.
    ISBN 0-87462-107-0

#24 Metaphysics and Ideology (1959) by Wm. Oliver Martin, Ph.D., professor of philosophy, University of Rhode Island.

ISBN 0-87462-124-0

#25 Language, Truth and Poetry (1960) by Victor M. Hamm, Ph.D., professor of English, Marquette University.

ISBN 0-87462-125-9

#26 Metaphysics and Historicity (1961) by Emil L. Fackenheim, Ph.D., professor of philosophy, University of Toronto.

ISBN 0-87462-126-7

#27 The Lure of Wisdom (1962) by James D. Collins, Ph.D., professor of philosophy, St. Louis University.

ISBN 0-87462-127-5

#28 Religion and Art (1963) by Paul Weiss, Ph.D. Sterling professor of philosophy, Yale University.

ISBN 0-87462-128-3

#29 St. Thomas and Philosophy (1964) by Anton C. Pegis, Ph.D., professor of philosophy, Pontifical Institute of Mediaeval Studies, Toronto.

ISBN 0-87462-129-1

#30 The University in Process (1965) by John O. Riedl, Ph.D., dean of faculty, Queensboro Community College.

ISBN 0-87462-130-5

#31 The Pragmatic Meaning of God (1966) by Robert O. Johann, associate professor of philosophy, Fordham University.

ISBN 0-87462-131-3

#32 Religion and Empiricism (1967) by John E. Smith, Ph.D., professor of philosophy, Yale University.

ISBN 0-87462-132-1

#50 Imagination and Metaphysics in St. Augustine (1986) by Robert J. O'Connell, S.J., professor of philosophy, Fordham University.
ISBN 0-87462-227-1

#51 Expectations of Immortality in Late Antiquity (1987) by A. Hilary Armstrong, former professor of classics and philosophy, Dalhousie University.
ISBN 0-87462-154-2

Uniform format, cover and binding.

Copies of this Aquinas Lecture and the others in the series are obtainable from:

Marquette University Press
Marquette University
Milwaukee, Wisconsin 53233, U.S.A.

Publishers of:

- Mediaeval Philosophical Texts in Translations
- Père Marquette Theology Lectures
- St. Thomas Aquinas Lectures